THE AMAZING PAPER CUTTINGS OF

HANS CHRISTIAN ANDERSEN

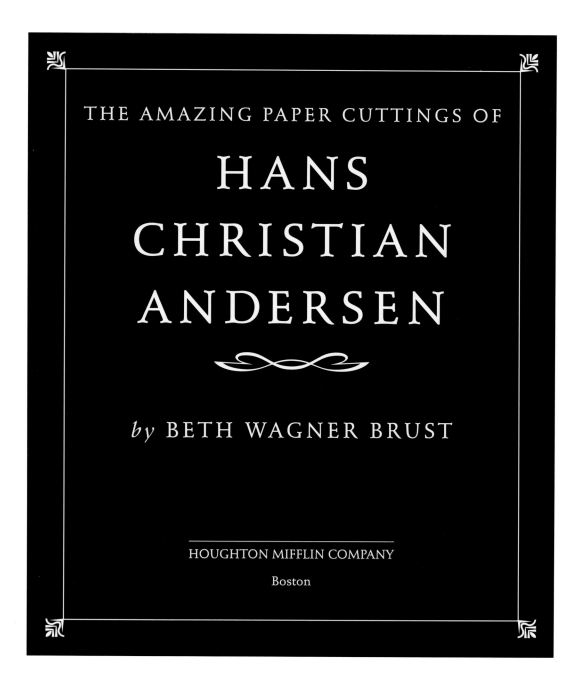

THE AMAZING PAPER CUTTINGS OF

HANS
CHRISTIAN
ANDERSEN

by BETH WAGNER BRUST

HOUGHTON MIFFLIN COMPANY

Boston

ACKNOWLEDGMENTS

I give my deepest gratitude to Erling Gormsbøl, assistant curator at The Hans Christian Andersen Museum in Odense, Denmark, for whom no question was too small and no request too big. I would also like to thank Birgitte Possing and Jacob Thomsen of The Royal Library in Copenhagen for providing cuttings from their departments' collections; and to Professor Johan de Mylius, Director of the Hans Christian Andersen International Research and Study Center at the University of Odense, for his expertise and critique of the manuscript.

The paper cuttings shown are made from white paper unless otherwise specified. When, where, and for whom a cutting was made has not always been recorded. The captions include all the information that is known.

Published by Houghton Mifflin Company, 222 Berkeley Street, Boston, Massachusetts 02116. Text copyright © 1994 by Beth Wagner Brust. All rights reserved. For information about permission to reproduce selections from this book, write to Permissions, Houghton Mifflin Company, 215 Park Avenue South, New York, New York 10003. Manufactured in the United States of America. Book design by David Saylor. The text of this book is set in 13 point Monotype Schneidler.
HOR 10 9 8 7 6 5 4 3 2

Library of Congress Cataloging-in-Publication Data

Brust, Beth Wagner.
The amazing paper cuttings of Hans Christian Andersen / by Beth Wagner Brust.
p. cm.
Includes bibliographic references and index.
ISBN 0-395-66787-9
1. Andersen, H. C. (Hans Christian), 1805–1875—Biography—Juvenile literature.
2. Silhouettes—Juvenile literature. [1. Andersen, H. C. (Hans Christian), 1805–1875.
2. Authors, Danish.] I. Title.
PT8119.A44 1994
839.8'136—dc20
[B]   93-24532   CIP   AC

FRONTISPIECE: *Smiling gentleman with crown of leaves.* 3 $\frac{1}{2}$" x 6 $\frac{1}{2}$".
The Hans Christian Andersen Museum, Odense.

To Sean and Pam, my traveling companions,

and to Paul, Ben, and Sallie, who stayed home.

Open square with pierrots riding on swans. Made in 1844 at Maxen estate in Saxony, Germany, for the Serre family. 9" x 9". The Hans Christian Andersen Museum, Odense.

Contents

THE AMAZING PAPER CUTTINGS OF

HANS CHRISTIAN ANDERSEN

Scene of dancers, flowers, and smiling faces. Cutting made for an auction in Copenhagen to raise money for families of Danish soldiers who fought against Prussia in 1864. The poem in the middle is in Danish: "This paper cut is somewhat dear / half a rigsdaler, *we'll say / But it's really a whole fairy tale / Your kind heart will have to pay."* 13 3/4" x 16 3/4". The Royal Library, Copenhagen.

Introduction

WRITER AND ARTIST

HANS CHRISTIAN ANDERSEN is known all over the world for his fairy tales. The Danish storyteller wrote "Thumbelina," "The Little Mermaid," "The Ugly Duckling," "The Emperor's New Clothes," "The Steadfast Tin Soldier," and more than 150 other stories. But many people who have enjoyed Andersen's fairy tales do not know that he was also an artist. Andersen taught himself to make drawings and collages, and he created puppets and puppet stages. He also cut wonderful pictures from pieces of paper. These paper cuttings enchanted everyone who saw them.

When Andersen was alive, from 1805 to 1875, people had to provide most of their own entertainment. Televisions, radios, and movies had not yet been invented. People could go to the theater or to concerts, but for amusement at home, they sang, played musical instruments, or played cards and games. They talked, read aloud, and told stories.

One of the best storytellers of his time, Andersen was called the "Fairy Tale Prince" by one young listener, and he was always in great demand as an entertainer. He told his stories aloud with lively gestures, and he wrote them in the language of daily life rather than in the formal language other Danish writers used at the time. This made his stories different from anyone else's. And like his fairy tales, Andersen's paper cuttings were highly original and greatly admired.

Andersen never explains in his writings how he became so skilled at making paper cuttings. Although he wrote constantly—diary entries, plays, poems, novels, travel books, an autobiography, and thousands of letters—he only rarely mentions paper cutting. Most of what is known about the cuttings comes from what other people wrote about Andersen and from what can be learned by looking at the paper cuttings themselves.

Andersen usually made his cuttings while people watched, often while he was telling a fairy tale aloud. Many of his listeners, especially the children, were so impressed by him that they remembered Andersen's paper cuttings and stories all their lives. Several of them wrote about Andersen and his amazing paper cuttings when they became adults.

The baroness Bodild von Donner was ten years old when she first heard Andersen tell his fairy tales and saw him make his cuttings at her family's home in Denmark. "He always cut with an enormous pair of paper scissors," she remembered as an adult. "It was a mystery to me how he could cut out such dainty, delicate things with his big hands and those enormous scissors."

Another of these children was Rigmor Bendix. She was Andersen's favorite goddaughter, so she had many opportunities to listen to Andersen's stories and watch him make cutouts. She later wrote, "While

Photograph of Hans Christian Andersen. Date unknown.
Stock Montage.

Andersen was talking he would fold a piece of paper, let the scissors run in and out in curves, then unfold the paper, and there the figures were."

In his cuttings and in his stories many of the same subjects appear: dancers, swans, elves, storks, palm trees, ballerinas, castles, devils, cupids, angels, mermaids, witches, and mosques. Yet Andersen never used the cutouts to illustrate his stories. When he told a story about a mermaid, for instance, he might cut out a picture of a theater stage. Perhaps he knew that the cutting would be even more intriguing if it was a surprise.

Although no one knows how many paper cuttings Andersen made, he created them from the time he was an adolescent until his death. Of the hundreds or perhaps thousands of cuttings he made, only about 250 have survived. Yet considering how fragile the cutouts are, it is surprising that so many still exist, particularly since most of them were given to young children to play with.

Now, over one hundred years after they were made, Andersen's paper cuttings continue to interest and amuse people. Each year more than 160,000 visitors go to The Hans Christian Andersen Museum in Odense, Denmark, to learn about Andersen's life and to admire the paper cuttings on display there.

Although he is remembered primarily as a writer, throughout his life Andersen also used scissors and paper as an outlet for his creative talents. In his cuttings he reveals both the fantastic world of his imagination and glimpses of his life.

A paper cutting that includes many of Andersen's favorite images: swans, palms, architectural elements, ladies with fans, and a "stealer of hearts" hanging from a gallows. 9" x 5 ½".
The Hans Christian Andersen Museum, Odense.

One

A CHILDHOOD OF PUPPETS
AND MAKE-BELIEVE

AS A CHILD, Hans Christian Andersen often walked through his neighborhood with his eyes closed. He grew up in the poorest section of Odense, a Danish town of five thousand people. Horse-drawn carriages thundered down narrow cobblestoned streets, drowning out the calls of street vendors advertising their wares. Cooking smells from open-hearth fires mingled with the stench of rotting garbage and open sewers. The children of poor working-class families had to pick their way through beggars, drunks, and stray dogs on the streets.

This rough section of Odense certainly was not a safe place for anyone to walk around blindly, but Hans Christian did it anyway. He wrote in his autobiography, "I was a singularly dreamy child and so constantly went about with my eyes shut." Even as a child, he set himself apart from the poverty-stricken world around him. "I will become famous," Andersen told his mother when he was fourteen years old. He had read about the lives of "extraordinary men," and he believed he understood how to become one: "First you go through a terribly hard time, and then you become famous," he said.

Born on April 2, 1805, Hans Christian Andersen was an only child and "extremely spoiled. . . . My father gratified me in all my wishes," Andersen wrote. "I possessed his whole heart; he lived for me." His father, also named Hans, was a shoemaker and a dreamer. His mother, Anne Marie, was a solid, practical woman who took care of him and kept their one-room home neat and clean. Andersen's grandmother, who lived nearby, visited often. She told him folktales and took him to parades and festivals.

The religious and folk beliefs he learned from his mother and grandmother are reflected in the witches, goblins, angels, and crosses that appear in some of Andersen's paper cuttings. After he grew up and studied at a university, he came to agree with his father that witches and goblins were "nonsense," but he included these characters in his stories and cuttings throughout his life.

Andersen was lucky to have a family that encouraged him to use his gifts. In his neighborhood, most children were expected to go to work at an early age. Most of them became factory workers or worked at a trade, which was what Andersen's father and grandfather, also a shoemaker, had been forced to do.

Andersen's father was bright and interested in learning. He had always wanted a good education, but his parents had been too poor to send him to a private grammar school. With only a charity school education, he was forced to learn a trade. He became a shoemaker, but all his life he hated and resented the job. Andersen's father wanted his son to be able to pursue his interests and dreams.

Hans Christian was afraid of his grandfather, who was mentally ill. As an old man, Andersen's grandfather walked around the countryside making strange wood carvings. He offered them as children's toys in exchange for food. Although he was harmless, boys used to chase and tease him. All his life Andersen feared that he might become insane like his grandfather. In both his father and grandfather, Andersen could see the unhappiness of two intelligent, creative people who became trapped by poverty and lack of education. He was determined not to be like them.

Unlike many of their neighbors, the Andersens owned a few books, which they kept in a cupboard over the workbench. Every night, the shoemaker read aloud Danish plays, stories from the Bible, and other literature. When Hans Christian learned to read at the charity school, he read and reread these same books. He especially loved the *Arabian Nights.* His many paper cuttings of Middle Eastern mosques may have been influenced by his memories of that book, although eventually he saw real mosques when he visited Turkey.

Andersen's father also made him toys, including a puppet theater. Together they made dolls and costumes, then acted out plays. In his auto-

Middle Eastern mosque with minarets. Made in 1859 at Nørre Vosborg manor for the Tang family. 7³/₄" x 5". The Hans Christian Andersen Museum, Odense.

biography, Andersen says that as a boy his "greatest delight" was making clothes for his dolls. Cutting out puppet clothes helped him develop the skills he later used for his paper cuttings.

When Andersen was seven years old, his parents took him to a real theater for the first time. He found the audience more interesting than the play at first, but after a few visits, the theater became his "favorite place." The Andersens could seldom afford tickets, but the boy made up plays and acted them out in his puppet theater. His love of the theater remained with him for his whole life, and many of his paper cuttings include stages, dancers, or theater clowns.

Andersen also enjoyed nature and the outdoors. On Sundays he went out with his father into the woods near town and collected strawberries or flowers. In his family's small backyard, he would make a little tent out of his mother's apron and lie underneath it, daydreaming and admiring the pattern that the leaves made against the sky.

When Andersen was eleven years old, his father died. His mother went out to work as a washerwoman at other people's houses, leaving Andersen on his own. When he was not in school, he usually stayed alone at home. He played with his little theater, made doll clothes, and read plays and other books.

Andersen discovered the works of William Shakespeare when he was about twelve years old. "I immediately acted out Shakespeare's plays on my little puppet theater," he recalled in his autobiography. "The more persons died in a play, the more interesting I thought it. At this time, I wrote my first piece." By the age of twelve, Hans Christian Andersen was already becoming what he would be for the rest of his life: a writer, a performer, and an artist.

Unlike many children, Andersen enjoyed playing alone. He liked his world of make-believe. "I very seldom played with other boys; even at

Coconut palm tree. Tree: 3" x 5 ¼". The Royal Library, Copenhagen.

school I took little interest in their games," he remembered. Andersen was always different from the other children, in his looks as well as in his interests. He was very tall and thin for his age, with long yellow hair, a long nose, and small green eyes—"tiny as green peas," he wrote in a poem. In another poem, he says that he looked like a scarecrow.

Although Andersen was unlike other children, he was neither shy nor afraid of people. On the contrary, he enjoyed performing in public, hoping to attract people's attention and praise. He would sing, in his beautiful high voice, down by the river or in his backyard, which was on the very edge of the town's poor section and next to the states-councillor's yard. He liked knowing that the "fine folks in the garden" next door were listening to him.

Andersen would also stand in the street and recite plays he had learned or poems he had written. There he read aloud his own first play "with great satisfaction and joy." But some of the neighbors were not as pleased with his performance as he was, and they made fun of him. Once, boys his age chased and teased him, shouting, "There runs the play-writer!"

When he turned fourteen, his mother decided he should start working, as was expected of boys his age. Since Andersen loved to collect colorful pieces of cloth to cut and sew, his mother thought he should be a tailor. But Hans Christian Andersen had greater ambitions than working at a trade. He wanted to be an actor at the Royal Theater in Copenhagen, the capital of Denmark.

Andersen's mother tried to persuade him not to leave Odense. She felt

Squatting man with curved shoes. 4 $\frac{1}{4}$" x 6 $\frac{3}{4}$". The H. Laage-Petersen Collection, The Royal Library, Copenhagen.

that Copenhagen was too big and too far away, and that he was too young to be on his own. Copenhagen is almost ninety miles from Odense—in those days a two-day journey by coach. But Andersen was determined. Finally his mother let him go, hoping that he would become frightened and return home in a few days.

So at fourteen years old, Hans Christian Andersen left his family and home in Odense and traveled to the great walled city of Copenhagen.

Two

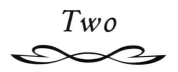

BECOMING A WRITER

ANDERSEN arrived in Denmark's capital on September 6, 1819. He brought with him ten Danish *rigsdalers* (which he spent in less than two weeks), a small bundle of clothes, and some stale bread. He knew no one in the city.

As soon as he found a place to stay, Andersen went to the Royal Theater. He tried to get an acting job but was told that he was too thin and awkward. Besides, the theater director said, the Royal Theater hired only educated people. Then Andersen tried to find work as a singer. He succeeded in charming a teacher into giving him free lessons, but six months later his adolescent voice began to crack and he could no longer sing.

Over the next two years, he continued to audition as a dancer and

Theater stage with ballerinas. 10 3/4" x 8 1/2". The Hans Christian Andersen Museum, Odense.

singer. His enthusiasm, sincerity, and persistence persuaded teachers to give him more lessons. They told him that with his limited talent and odd looks, he could only be in the chorus.

Finally, Andersen became part of the walk-on cast for ballets and plays. When a crowd of people appeared in a scene, he would be among them. Barely earning enough money to survive, he spent his free time building a puppet theater like the one his father had built for him. He begged shopkeepers for scraps of silk and velvet, and, as he had done at home, he sewed clothes for his puppets.

In 1822, Andersen was fired from his job, but he was determined to remain in the theater. It was then that he first considered writing as a possible career. "It was absolutely necessary that I should write a piece for the theatre, and that [it] *must* be accepted," he later wrote. "There was no other salvation for me." He based his first play on some of the pieces he had invented for his puppet theater.

Without formal education, Andersen could not write a play suitable for the stage. The Royal Theater rejected his first plays, but the board of directors recognized his talent as a storyteller. They told Andersen they hoped that, with more education, he might "some time, be able to write a work which should be worthy of being acted on the Danish stage."

One of the directors, Jonas Collin, arranged for Andersen to receive a royal grant to go to a small-town grammar school. Andersen gratefully accepted the offer to get the kind of education that he could never have afforded otherwise. Yet going back to school was difficult for him. He had hoped to be an actor, a singer, or a writer—instead he was a schoolboy. Seventeen years old and as tall as a full-grown man, he had to study with the school's twelve-year-olds. Even worse, the headmaster constantly criticized and teased him. After five years of hard work, he completed his elementary and secondary education in 1827. He then returned to Copenhagen, where he soon entered the university.

Andersen began his writing career in earnest while still a college student. By 1831 he had published his first books, including a humorous book about his walks in Copenhagen and a book of poetry. Two years later, after publishing several plays and more books of poetry, he received another royal grant, this one for travel to other countries. His tour of Europe was the first of his twenty-nine trips abroad.

When he returned to Copenhagen, Andersen completed his first novel. While he was waiting for it to be published, he began the work that was to make him famous. "I have started on some 'Tales Told to Children,' and seem to be making good progress with them," he wrote to some friends. "I have done a couple of stories I remember having liked when little, and that I think are not generally known. I have written them exactly as I would tell them to a child. I want to win the coming generations, you see."

In May 1835, four of his fairy tales were published as a book called *Wonderful Stories for Children*. Three of the stories—"The Tinder Box," "Little Claus and Big Claus," and "The Princess on the Pea"—were retellings of traditional tales. The fourth Andersen had made up himself. Titled "Little Ida's Flowers," it was originally told to Ida Thiele, the daugh-

Men in a circle holding hearts and hands. 8 ¹/₄" x 8". The H. Laage-Petersen Collection, The Royal Library, Copenhagen.

ter of a young professor who had befriended Andersen during his first year in Copenhagen.

The story was Andersen's answer to a question the little girl asked him one day when he was visiting the family. Ida had showed him a bouquet of faded flowers. Why had her beautiful flowers faded overnight? she asked. Andersen explained that the flowers had been dancing the night before and had stayed out very late, which made them tired and faded.

"Little Ida's Flowers" was Andersen's first published original fairy tale

Dancing pierrot. Made for Mathilde Ørsted, daughter of physicist H. C. Ørsted. 6 ¹/₂" x 8 ³/₄". The Hans Christian Andersen Museum, Odense.

and it includes his first written mention of paper cutting. In the story a college student cuts out paper figures to amuse a little girl. Near the beginning of the story, Andersen writes: "She was very fond of him because he knew the most lovely stories and could cut out such amusing pictures—hearts with little dancing ladies inside them, flowers, and great castles with doors that opened. He was a very jolly student!"

Andersen wished everyone would respond to his stories and his cuttings as Ida does. But later in the story, an old man criticizes the student:

Two people hanging from a heart gallows. Made in 1856 on the Maxen estate in Saxony, Germany, for the Serre family. 2 ¹/₂" x 3 ³/₄". The Hans Christian Andersen Museum, Odense.

31

"He didn't like the student and always used to grumble when he saw him cutting out those comical pictures—sometimes it was a man hanging from a gibbet, with a heart in his hand because he was a stealer of hearts; sometimes an old witch riding on a broomstick, with her husband perched on the bridge of her nose. The Councillor didn't like it, and so he would say, as he said now: 'What nonsense is this to put into a child's head! All stuff and nonsense.'"

Andersen invented a character who criticizes his paper cuttings, but as far as anyone knows, no one ever did criticize them. Some people told him that his fairy tales were silly and childish and that he should write only serious literature, but everyone seems to have loved his paper cutouts.

Three

HANS CHRISTIAN ANDERSEN
AT CENTER STAGE

Y NEED TO BE NOTICED is so great," wrote Hans Christian Andersen in his diary in 1841.

Even though his hopes of a stage career were dashed early on, he still loved the theater. He often saw two or three plays in one night, and he wrote forty-seven plays. But seeing or writing plays wasn't the same as being on the stage and the focus of everyone's attention.

With his paper cutting and story telling, Andersen found a way to perform that would satisfy his need to be noticed. He would arrange his audience of children and adults around him in a circle, either sitting or standing. When everyone was quiet, he would begin.

Edvard Collin, Jonas Collin's son, once described Andersen's lively story telling: "He didn't say, 'The children got into the carriage and then drove away.' No, he said, 'They got into the carriage—"good-bye, Dad! good-bye, Mum!"—the whip cracked smack! smack! and away they went, come on! gee-up!'"

In the words he chose and in the way he spoke them, Andersen was a wonderful storyteller.

Woman in fancy dress. Made in Copenhagen for Louise Cruse, daughter of newspaper editor A. P. Livnge. Cut from a concert program. 4 ³/₄" x 4 ¹/₂". The Hans Christian Andersen Museum, Odense.

Four girls holding a floral hoop. Made in the 1850s for Mathilde Ørsted, daughter of physicist H. C. Ørsted. 8 ½" x 5 ¼". The Hans Christian Andersen Museum, Odense.

Making a paper cutting while he was telling a story kept his audience even more riveted to his performance. Not only did they want to know how the story ended, they wanted to see what the cutting would look like. When Andersen would open up the folded paper to reveal elves and swans or pixies and clowns, his audience was always thrilled.

During one of Andersen's trips to Germany, he visited the home of the painter Wilhelm von Kaulbach, who later described how the famous author entertained them: "When he had finished his tale, he would spread a whole string of ballet dancers in front of us. Andersen would be delighted with the success of his work. He enjoyed our praise of it more than the impression made on us by his story."

Why would such a successful writer care more about people's reactions to his paper artwork than about their reactions to his stories? One answer might be that Andersen knew that his fairy tales were popular. Everywhere he went, people thanked him for publishing his stories or begged him to tell one. But his paper cuttings were unknown to many people, so he could surprise them with his skillful handling of scissors and paper.

In addition to his love of attention and praise, there may be another reason why compliments meant so much to him. Andersen was able to accomplish something that was almost impossible in the early nineteenth century. Born and raised in "the swamp," as he called the slums of Odense, he gained acceptance in upper-class society. In his diary he frequently wrote about mingling with dukes and duchesses, lords and ladies, and even kings and queens.

Although Andersen was witty, educated, and famous, he never felt equal to his well-born friends. "I had and still have a feeling," he wrote in his autobiography, "as though I were a poor peasant lad over whom a royal mantle is thrown." He often felt alone and like an outsider. His cuttings, like his stories, charmed his audiences and helped dissolve the barriers that, he felt, stood between him and his new friends. When telling stories and making paper cuttings he was doing the two things he did better than anyone else he knew.

Clowns, sun, and theater. Made in 1865 at Frijsenborg Manor for the family of Count Frijsenborg.
Privately owned.

Pierrot with tree, angel, and dancer. Made on the Bregentved estate. 3 ½" x 5 ¼". The Hans Christian Andersen Museum, Odense.

Andersen also felt he needed to make up for his unattractive appearance. When Edvard Collin wrote to Andersen, accusing him of being too eager to recite for people, Andersen replied: "Since I cannot please with my appearance I take refuge in whatever is at hand." If he could not be handsome, at least he could please people by entertaining them.

Making paper cuttings while telling stories entertained Andersen, along with his audience. As his writings became well known, he received many invitations to dine at people's homes. Night after night, he found himself an honored guest at manor houses, large estates, and grand castles, where he was always asked to tell his fairy tales.

In the houses where he knew the children, Andersen would go straight to the nursery to tell them a few stories before dinner. According to one Andersen biographer, "He could sit there for hours, telling fairy tales and cutting out his well-known paper figures."

After dinner, he would be asked to tell stories for the family and guests. Andersen sometimes used these occasions to try out new stories or to improve stories he was preparing for publication, but some tales he told over and over again because they were so popular. Making a paper cutting at the same time kept him from being bored.

Trees with stork and dancer. Made in the 1860s for Axeline Lund, wife of the painter
F. C. Lund. 4 ¼" x 5 ¼". The Hans Christian Andersen Museum, Odense.

Four

"TO TRAVEL IS TO LIVE"

In a letter to a friend, Andersen wrote, "For me, to travel is to live." As one of the most well-traveled men of his day, he often compared himself to the long-legged stork, symbol of travel and rootlessness. Every year, during the warm spring months, storks nested in the chimneys of the same Danish neighborhoods. In the fall they would migrate to Africa. Andersen, too, usually left Denmark in the fall to avoid the cold, wet winter, and he returned in the spring. Storks often appear in his cuttings and in his fairy tales.

"It is only when travelling that life becomes rich and vital," he wrote. "I must see and see again. I cannot do anything else than pack whole towns, tribes, mountains, and seas into my mind." Seeing new places and experiencing other cultures sparked Andersen's creativity, providing inspiration for his writing and his cuttings. As a child Andersen had sometimes closed his eyes to the world, yet throughout his life he looked around him with an artist's vision.

He even saw cuttings in new surroundings. In the English city of York, for example, there is a huge cathedral with soaring arches and heavily decorated steeples. After Andersen toured it, he noted in his diary that it was "magnificent like a cutout."

Although most of his cutouts were based on things he had imagined rather than on things he had seen, Andersen occasionally used his skill with scissors like a camera, in order to capture a scene that he wanted to remember. He used paper cutting in this way when he first visited Italy. It was 1833, and the camera was still in the process of being invented. In Rome Andersen met the internationally known Danish sculptor Bertel Thorvaldsen, and they quickly became good friends.

One day, Andersen was invited to watch a French artist, Horace Vernet, paint Thorvaldsen's portrait. At some point during the session, Andersen must have pulled out his traveling scissors and a piece of paper, because he cut a portrait of his friend.

The cutting looks crude and unfinished, but it is not. Placed side by side, Vernet's finished oil portrait and Andersen's cutting show Thorvaldsen in the same pose, wearing the same high-collared shirt, and standing next to the same bust.

The Thorvaldsen cutting was rediscovered just as the Hans Christian

LEFT: *Cutout portrait of sculptor Bertel Thorvaldsen. Made in 1833 in Rome, at the studio of French painter Horace Vernet.* 2 ½" x 2 ¾". The Hans Christian Andersen Museum, Odense.

RIGHT: *Vernet's portrait of Thorvaldsen. 1833, Rome. Oil paint on canvas.* 30" x 40". Thorvaldsen Museum, Copenhagen.

Andersen Museum opened an exhibition about Andersen's travels in Italy. Vernet's portrait of Thorvaldsen was included. A Danish family had contacted the museum to say that they had a cutting in their possession. The museum curators recognized it as Andersen's portrait of Thorvaldsen in Vernet's studio. The museum bought the cutting in 1990, and it is now part of their permanent collection. New Andersen cuttings continue to be discovered in ways similar to this.

While Andersen was traveling, he found yet another use for his paper cuttings. He could pull out scissors and paper to help him communicate with other travelers who didn't speak Danish and whose language he didn't understand. One such episode was noted by Sir William Ainsworth, a British explorer, in 1841.

The day before Andersen was to leave a Turkish town across the harbor from Constantinople (now Istanbul), he received bad news. "Today letters from Cairo and Constantinople report that two hundred people daily are dying of the plague," Andersen wrote in his diary. Cholera had broken out—a highly contagious disease that can easily kill its victims.

Andersen traveled on the ship through several countries before being stopped for ten days at the Hungarian border. Along with hundreds of other travelers, he was isolated in a camp at Orsova and was watched to make sure that he did not carry the deadly disease.

His roommate, Sir Ainsworth, noted that Andersen "had a talent for communicating with his fellow internees by means of drawings and paper cuts of his experiences earlier in the journey." One of Andersen's cuttings was of Turkish "whirling dervishes," Muslim holy men who wore big skirts and tall hats and were known for their religious custom of spinning around and around until they fell into a trance. Ainsworth was so impressed by the images that he claimed to have used Andersen's cuttings as the basis for drawings of the dervishes in his own book.

Andersen's paper cuttings again bridged a communication gap when he traveled to England to stay with Charles Dickens. The famous author of *Oliver Twist, Great Expectations, A Christmas Carol,* and other classics had

Gnomes and ballerinas on a hoop. Made in 1859 at Nørre Vosborg Manor for the Tang family.
4 $^1/_4$" x 8 $^1/_4$". The Hans Christian Andersen Museum, Odense.

met Andersen in 1847 when Andersen first visited England. They admired each other's work and wrote to each other regularly over the next ten years. Finally, in 1857, Dickens persuaded Andersen to return to England and visit him and his family at their home outside London.

While Andersen and Dickens had much in common, they could not overcome the language barrier. Although they had been able to write to each other in English, Andersen did not speak the language well, and Dickens spoke no Danish. After one conversation, in which Andersen had done his best to talk in English, Dickens joked to him, "You had better speak Danish; I think I could understand you better."

But Andersen could still communicate through his paper cuttings. On the second day of the visit, Andersen noted in his diary, "I was a great success after dinner with my cutouts." Although the visit became more and more difficult as it stretched to five weeks, Andersen impressed the family, especially the children, with his fascinating paper figures.

One of the sons, Henry Dickens, was eight years old at the time of Andersen's visit. He later wrote about it in his memoirs, calling their guest "a lovable and yet a somewhat uncommon and strange personality." But he also remembered that Andersen "had one beautiful accomplishment, which was the cutting out in paper, with an ordinary pair of scissors, of lovely little figures of sprites and elves, gnomes, fairies and animals of all kinds, which might well have stepped out of the pages of his books. These figures turned out to be quite delightful in their refinement and delicacy in design and touch."

Charles Dickens later mentioned in a letter to a friend that his guest "cut out paper into all sorts of patterns." In the same letter, Dickens describes how Andersen had been riding in a cab in London when he became afraid that he would be robbed. He hid his money, his watch, and a few other things—including a pair of scissors—in his boots for safekeeping. Wherever he went, Andersen seems to have traveled with scissors.

Back in Copenhagen, Andersen sometimes used memories of his travels as the basis for cuttings. His tranquil scene of a large sailing ship, the *Galathea,* is one of these. The ship is shown at anchor in the harbor of Constantinople. A Danish captain, Steen Bille, had sailed the *Galathea* around the world from 1845 to 1847, and in 1851 wrote a book about his adventures.

Sailing ship Galathea.
Made for Steen Bille, the ship's captain. 2" x 1 3/4".
The Portman Collection,
The Royal Library, Copenhagen.

Andersen had met Bille, and he was so moved by the book that he made a cutting based on his own knowledge of Turkey. While a visitor there, Andersen had written: "The mountains behind Constantinople had snow on them in the clear, warm sunshine. . . . The Sea of Marmara was like glass. . . . Ships with all their sails were lying at anchor like swans mirroring themselves in the water; the small boats were gliding like black snakes across the current."

His cutting of the *Galathea* captures that same feeling of a ship floating on a calm sea, by an exotic and beautiful city. As always, Andersen's travels inspired him in his art.

THE GOOD
"CUTTING-OUT PLACES"

LTHOUGH HE LOVED CHILDREN and enjoyed being with them, Hans Christian Andersen never married or had children of his own. He never owned a house. Even when he was not touring Denmark or other parts of Europe, he moved around Copenhagen, living in rented apartments or in hotels. He also stayed in the countryside, a guest in other people's homes for weeks or months at a time. He envied his friends' family lives and liked to spend time with their children.

As much as he loved to travel, Andersen still needed to feel at home somewhere part of the time. "As people grow older," he wrote in his auto-biography, "however much they may be tossed about in the world, some one place must be the true home; even the bird of passage has one fixed

Windmill man dangling a dancer.
Made for Louise Drewsen,
daughter of Edvard Collin.
3 ¹/₄" x 4 ¹/₄". The Hans Christian
Andersen Museum, Odense.

spot to which it hastens: mine was and is the house of my friend Collin."

Jonas Collin, who had arranged for Andersen's scholarship to the private grammar school, always kept his home in Copenhagen open to Andersen. Collin was a second father to Andersen, and even after he had completed his schooling he continued to ask Collin's advice on financial, career, and personal matters. Andersen described him as "one of the men

Sunflower man. Made in 1848 in the village of Sorø, Denmark, for Johan Martin Christian Lange. 5 ½" x 8 ¾". The Portman Collection, The Royal Library, Copenhagen.

who do more than they promise."

Collin, his wife, and their five children made Hans Christian Andersen feel like part of the family. "Treated as a son, almost grown up with the children," he once wrote about his relationship with the Collins, "I have become a member of the family. . . . A better home have I never known." Over time, Andersen became like an uncle to Jonas Collin's grandchildren and great-grandchildren. Andersen called the Collin home one of the good "cutting-out places," his name for houses where he felt particularly inspired to make paper cuttings.

One of Jonas Collin's great-granddaughters, Rigmor Bendix, wrote: "When he could give us children pleasure, he never neglected the opportunity to do so. He presented his fairy tales to us, took us to the theatre . . . but what interested us most of all were the figures he cut out, and which he often pasted into the scrapbooks."

Andersen made thirteen scrapbooks for his favorite children, many of them Collin's young relatives. Onto the pages of a blank book he pasted his own cuttings, usually made of brightly colored paper, along with pictures he had cut from magazines, advertisements, printed sheets, postcards, and wrapping paper.

These scrapbooks were special. In nineteenth-century Denmark, few picture books were published for children, and of those only a few were in color. In peasant cottages, there were seldom any books other than the Bible, a hymnal, and perhaps a book of sermons. Even in the homes of wealthier families, there were no children's books meant for entertainment. Books for children were supposed to train them in good manners and proper living.

What made Andersen's scrapbooks so wonderful is that they were pure fun. Besides the colorful cuttings and pictures, he wrote little poems in the books. Some of them were about paper cutting. In the scrapbook he made for Astrid Stampe, another Collin great-granddaughter, he wrote:

In Andersen's paper-cuts you see
His poetry!
A medley of diverting treasures
All done with scissors.

Another good cutting-out place was Holsteinborg, which Andersen described as "a comfortable, old castle, surrounded by forest" near the Baltic Sea. Countess Mimi von Holstein had known Andersen since her childhood. She pampered Andersen by sending a heated carriage to his doorstep in winter to bring him to the castle, where she would give him the best guest room. In return, Andersen made many paper cuttings for

Two pairs of dancing figures. Made in 1848–49 for the children of an artist, Jens Adolf Jerichau.
7" x 3 3/4". The Hans Christian Andersen Museum, Odense.

her other guests and especially for her two children.

The countess's daughter, Baroness Bodild von Donner, later wrote about Andersen and his cuttings. She said, "When I was a child I was delighted when he cut out chains of little dolls in white paper that I could stand on the table and blow so they moved forward." They glided across the surface as if they were dancing across a ballroom floor. Sometimes her mother pasted Andersen's paper cuttings onto her lamp shade. With the bright light behind them, the figures stood out beautifully.

During a visit to Holsteinborg in the spring of 1874, Andersen got to know a local clergyman's daughter, Elisabeth Møller, who spent several days there. Before dinner one evening, Andersen presented her with a bouquet of flowers that he had picked. Then he decided that the bouquet needed a paper holder around the middle to keep the stems together. As Møller later wrote, "He took a pair of scissors and paper from his pocket and cut it out while I watched." Only someone who planned to make cuttings often would carry scissors and paper in his pocket!

Although Andersen made some cuttings for adults, they were usually for children. But sometimes parents or other adults were so captivated by Andersen's artistry that they took away the cuttings to preserve them.

For example, in his travel book on Sweden, Andersen recalled how an innkeeper's granddaughter came to his room soon after his arrival. He "quickly cut out for her from a sheet of paper a Turkish mosque with minarets and open windows." Moments later, he heard excited voices outside and quietly stepped out onto the balcony. "I saw Grandmother down

Bouquet holder and butterfly with dancers. The Danish words on the bouquet holder mean "Cut by H. C. Andersen at Holsteinborg, 1874—Given with a bouquet to Elisabeth Møller." The butterfly would have been used to decorate the bouquet. The holder and the butterfly together measure 5 $\frac{1}{4}$" x 4 $\frac{1}{2}$".
The H. Laage-Petersen Collection, The Royal Library, Copenhagen.

in the yard, holding my paper cutting up and beaming," he wrote. "A crowd . . . stood around, all in an ecstasy about my work, while the child, the blessed little child, was crying and holding her hands up for her lawful property which she was not allowed to keep because it was so nice."

The paper cuttings served other purposes besides entertaining his friends. Andersen often made them as gifts to thank people for their hospitality. Although his stories were a type of gift, the cuttings could be left behind as tangible tokens of his affection for his hosts and their other guests. People valued his cuttings because they were made by a famous writer, and because each was unique. Andersen used many of the same images in his cuttings, but no two were identical.

The paper cuttings also solved the problem of what Andersen might give his friends and their children for their birthdays and Christmas. He could be generous, but in general the cost of things worried him. His travel diaries frequently mention how much a carriage ride cost, how much he tipped a servant, how much he paid for flowers, and so on. Andersen was afraid that he might become poor again in his old age, despite an annual pension from the king of Denmark and a good yearly income.

Paper cuttings made perfect gifts. They were made of whatever paper was around, usually thin, white writing paper. They cost him almost nothing, yet his friends treasured them. His very wealthy friends could afford to buy themselves almost anything they wanted, but Andersen could give them something that was not for sale.

Some of Andersen's cuttings were gifts that served a particular purpose. He made bookmarks, colorful Christmas tree ornaments, and bouquet holders. Once he even made paper patterns for cutting out cookies. In his day, people would place paper patterns on the dough and cut around them if they didn't have cookie cutters. Still, most of his cuttings were for decoration or for play.

One of Andersen's most stunning birthday-gift cuttings is the beautiful piece he made for Marie Steenbuch. She was the daughter of the local doctor for the area around Holsteinborg, where Andersen stayed during May and June 1874. The Steenbuchs were invited to dinner to celebrate Marie's fourth birthday. Andersen made a lovely, lacelike cutting for her.

Andersen had just turned sixty-nine that April, and he was already suffering from cancer of the liver, which would take his life a year later. He showed remarkable steadiness and patience to make such a delicate, complex cutting. Andersen was always willing to make an effort to please people, especially children.

"Marie" with flowers. Made in 1874 at Holsteinborg for Marie Steenbuch's fourth birthday.
6 ³/₄" x 5 ¹/₄". The H. Laage-Petersen Collection, The Royal Library, Copenhagen.

Six

THE ART OF PAPER CUTTING

AKING PAPER CUTTINGS is not always easy, but Andersen made it look that way. Describing her godfather at work, Rigmor Bendix said: "Without any special effort, he cut out the most marvellous figures, and their expression was always striking. He never drew them, but whilst he was sitting talking to us he folded the paper together, and, without the slightest thing to go by, he merrily cut away—and there was the idea, true to life."

Just as Andersen broke new ground when he wrote his fairy tales in the language of daily life, he ignored the paper-cutting styles of his day and invented an informal, striking style. Some of his cuttings were delicate and complex, some were chunky and simple, but all of them differed greatly from the typical silhouette or "outline" cuttings popular in Europe in the eighteenth and nineteenth centuries.

Paper cutting is an extremely ancient art form. It began almost two thousand years ago in China, where paper was invented before A.D. 200, and it is still popular in China, Germany, Poland, and Mexico. In Andersen's time, however, Europeans did not know about Chinese paper cuttings. Instead, they patterned their silhouettes after ancient Greek silhouettes. These Greek silhouettes were not paper cuttings, but paintings of black, shadowlike figures.

The Industrial Revolution, which began in 1760 in England, had helped make paper cuttings affordable. Factories with large machines began to replace the older, slower processes of making things by hand. Even paper and scissors were expensive until they could be made in factories. As soon as these materials became inexpensive, silhouette cutting became the rage in Europe.

If people couldn't afford to have an artist paint their portrait, having a silhouette made enabled them to have their likeness recorded for their family and future generations. The technique became so popular that some people who could afford to have their portraits painted also had silhouettes made. Their popularity lasted until the 1860s, when cameras became common and photographic portraits became fashionable.

Hans Christian Andersen's cuttings were very different from silhouettes. Silhouettists used black paper. Andersen never did. He usually cut from white paper, though sometimes he used colored paper. Silhouettists

Traditional silhouette of Hans Christian Andersen and the Swedish opera singer Jenny Lind. Cut from black paper. Artist unknown. Courtesy of The New-York Historical Society.

usually drew a pattern to follow before they began cutting. Andersen did not. As Rigmor Bendix observed, he simply folded and cut the paper. There are no pencil or pen lines on any of his cuttings, not even on the more complex ones.

Another important difference is that traditional silhouettists almost always cut realistic portraits of their subjects in profile. Andersen made fantasy figures that usually faced the viewer straight on. Occasionally, he cut profile images of a long-nosed man (possibly a self-portrait) and witches, but most of his cuttings show a front view of his subject.

Finally, traditional silhouettists usually cut quiet, serious portraits of people. Andersen's cuttings were rarely serious. His images are whimsical, fantastic, funny, sad, or scary, and they are always full of energy and life.

In keeping with his untraditional and inventive approach to cutting, Andersen experimented with new materials from time to time. When he wanted to make a cutting for Louise Cruse, the daughter of a newspaper editor, he looked for an interesting article in her father's paper, the *Copenhagen Post*. After finding a story about Brazil, Andersen cut out a piece of the newspaper into the figure of a man. He imagined how he thought a Brazilian might look and even centered the word *Brazilien* on the brim of the man's hat.

Andersen also made cuttings from concert programs, old letters and manuscripts, and even the leaves of a rubber tree.

Looking closely at the paper cuttings, it is possible to discover some of Andersen's techniques. Crease marks show where he folded the paper, while an absence of creases shows that he cut without folding it. Some of Andersen's cuttings were "single cuts" made from a flat sheet of paper. His swans, dancing clowns, and storks are all flat-paper cuttings.

Most of his pieces are "double cuts." By folding the paper in half, he created a simple symmetry: whatever appears on one side also appears on

LEFT: *"Brazilian" newspaper man. Made in 1830 in Copenhagen for Louise Cruse. Cut from newspaper.* 4 3/4" x 7 1/2". The Hans Christian Andersen Museum, Odense.

RIGHT: *Man and woman. Made for the Melchior family. Cut from rubber tree leaf.* 3 1/4" x 6 3/4". The Hans Christian Andersen Museum, Odense.

the other. He used this one-fold technique for heads, human figures, theater stages, buildings with doors in the middle, linked figures like a pair of dancing girls or boys, and so on.

Sometimes Andersen folded the paper twice, making four sections that

Scene of dancers, pierrots, and sandmen. An example of a two-fold cutting. Made for Ingeborg Drewsen, daughter of Jonas Collin. 5 $\frac{1}{2}$" x 8 $\frac{1}{4}$". The Hans Christian Andersen Museum, Odense.

meet in the center. In some of these two-fold cuttings, Andersen made the same images appear in all four sections, but often he folded the paper, cut, then refolded the paper at different points and cut again to vary the images in the four sections.

The two-fold technique enabled Andersen to make some of his largest and most beautiful paper cuttings. One of these he called a "whole fairy tale," because he had included so many of his fanciful figures in it.

Unfinished large cutting.
13 $\frac{1}{2}$" x 16 $\frac{3}{4}$". The Hans Christian
Andersen Museum, Odense.

It is possible to find out how he made some of these bigger cuttings by studying one of his unfinished large paper cuttings. The small hole in the center design on the right suggests that Andersen had started with the most complicated part of the design when the paper tore. Starting with the hardest part of the design is a common paper cutting technique. First, cutting from a firm piece of solid paper is easier than cutting from a limp piece of paper with holes in it. Also, if the paper-cutting artist were to make a mistake in the most difficult parts, he or she would not have wasted time and effort on the simpler sections.

Another large two-fold cutting is the piece he made for his friend, Dorothea Melchior. In it Andersen included most of his favorite images: angels, ballerinas, windmill men with heart-shaped windows, the Sandman, bakers, and swans.

The Melchiors, a wealthy Danish merchant family, had become good friends with Andersen in his later years. They had a house in Copenhagen and a country villa that became one of Andersen's good cutting-out places. When, in the last months of his life, Andersen needed constant care, Mrs. Melchior and a servant nursed him at the country estate. There he died on August 4, 1875, at the age of seventy.

The year before he died, Andersen made his last large cutting as a gift for Mrs. Melchior. Its grim images—skulls and frowning death masks—do not appear in any other known cutting. They reflect the artist's poor health and his knowledge of his approaching death. At the center of the piece there is also a cross, an image seldom seen in his cuttings even though Andersen was a religious man.

One paper-cutting expert has said that the most important thing about a cutting is neither the style nor the separate images, but the overall design and how the figures are positioned. The cuttings of Hans Christian Andersen are balanced and well designed, even though he had never had any instruction and he never drew the design before cutting. He was an artist of great talent and originality.

Andersen's last large cutting. Made in 1874 at Rolighed, the Melchiors' country villa, for Dorothea Melchior. 10 1/2" x 16 3/4".
The Hans Christian Andersen Museum, Odense.

Pierrot balancing a tray of objects on his head. Made at Borreby, a medieval castle near Basnaes Manor, for the Carstenschiold family. 5 ¼" x 5 ". The Hans Christian Andersen Museum, Odense.

Conclusion

DARING TO BE DIFFERENT

O NE OF ANDERSEN'S best-known paper cuttings is of a theater clown called a *pierrot* holding a tray on his head. Some people say it represents a street vendor selling figurines. Others believe the five images on the tray represent places and things that Andersen associated with his life.

The building on the far left resembles Andersen's birthplace. The shape next to that looks like the grammar school in Slagelse, where he was sent for his formal education. At the center is a windmill much like the hundreds of mills that dotted the Danish countryside in Andersen's day and were used to grind wheat into flour. To the right of the windmill is a tall church steeple, which may represent St. Knud (Saint Canute's) Church in Odense where Andersen was confirmed at the age of fourteen.

Finally, on the far right is a swan. When Hans Christian Andersen wrote his tale about the ugly duckling, he might have been writing about himself. All his life Andersen felt ugly because of his big nose, small eyes, and tall, skinny body. When he was young, he never felt he fit in with the other children, just as the ugly duckling never fit in with the other ducks. But like the ugly duckling that grew up to discover itself a swan, Andersen, despite his odd looks and unusual interests, discovered that he was witty, intelligent, and charming. The swan became one of his favorite symbols.

As a writer, Hans Christian Andersen forged a new style in his fairy tales. He avoided the flowery language used by the authors of the time, even those writing for children. Instead, he wrote in conversational Danish, which no other author had ever dared use in a book.

As an artist, Andersen also forged a new style. Just as lively, dramatic, and original as his tales, his cuttings broke with tradition. He invented a new approach to an ancient art form. The results were whimsical, charming paper cuttings that enchanted people of all ages wherever he went.

Through his little-known talent for making delightful paper cuttings, the well-known Hans Christian Andersen proved that he was an accomplished artist as well as an author. And through these cuttings, as much as through his fairy tales, he was able to express himself and his private world of make-believe. Andersen dared to be different—with words and with scissors—and, as a result, created works of art that can be enjoyed as much today as they were more than one hundred years ago.

Fellow with earhoop and boots. (Figure originally had two earhoops but has been damaged.)
5 ¼" x 8 ¼". The Hans Christian Andersen Museum, Odense.

Bibliography and Source Notes

The following books and articles provided valuable information for this book. Some of these same sources will be of interest to readers who wish to know more about Hans Christian Andersen or the art of paper cutting. Books marked with an asterisk can be easily read by young people.

General

Four books were especially helpful to the author, who referred to them for almost every chapter. The first two are about Hans Christian Andersen's life. The latter two are about Andersen's artwork.

Andersen, Hans Christian. *The Fairy Tale of My Life: An Autobiography*. New York: Paddington Press, Ltd., 1975 (Reprint of 1871 English edition).

Bredsdorff, Elias. *Hans Christian Andersen: The Story of His Life and Work 1805–1875*. New York: Charles Scribner's Sons, 1975.

Heltoft, Kjeld. *Hans Christian Andersen as an Artist*. Translated by Reginald Spink. Copenhagen: The Royal Danish Ministry of Foreign Affairs, Rosenkilde og Bagger, 1977.

de Mylius, Johan. *H. C. Andersen Paper Cuts*. Copenhagen: Komma & Clausen, 1992.

Introduction

The Andersen-Scudder Letters: Hans Christian Andersen's Correspondence with Horace Scudder. Edited and translated by Jean Hersholt and Waldemar Westergaard. Berkeley & Los Angeles: University of California Press, 1949.

One

Böök, Fredrik. *Hans Christian Andersen: A Biography*. Translated by George C. Schoolfield. Norman: University of Oklahoma Press, 1962.

Spink, Reginald. *Hans Christian Andersen and His World*. New York: G. P. Putnam's Sons, 1972.

Two

*Harboe, Paul. *A Child's Story of Hans Christian Andersen*. New York: Duffield & Co., 1907.

Nielsen, Erling. *Hans Christian Andersen (1805–1875)*. Copenhagen: The Royal Danish Ministry of Foreign Affairs, 1983.

Spink. *Hans Christian Andersen and His World*.

Three

Böök. *Hans Christian Andersen.*

The Diaries of Hans Christian Andersen. Edited and translated by Patricia L. Conroy and Sven H. Rossel. Seattle: University of Washington Press, 1990.

*Godden, Rumer. *Hans Christian Andersen: A Great Life in Brief.* New York: Alfred A. Knopf, 1955.

Reumert, Elith. *Hans Andersen the Man.* Translated by Jessie Bröchner. London: Tower Books, Methuen & Co., 1927. Reprint. Detroit: Tower Books, 1971.

Four

Andersen, Hans Christian. *A Poet's Bazaar: A Picturesque Tour in Germany, Italy, Greece, and the Orient.* Boston: Houghton, Osgood, and Company, 1879.

The Andersen-Scudder Letters.

Bendix, Rigmor. "Hans Christian Andersen—His Methods of Amusing Children." *The Strand Magazine,* June 1905.

The Diaries of Hans Christian Andersen.

Five

*Andersen, Hans Christian and Grandfather Drewsen. *Christine's Picture Book.* New York: Holt, Rinehart and Winston, 1984.

The Andersen—Scudder Letters.

Bendix. "Hans Christian Andersen—His Methods of Amusing Children."

Böök. *Hans Christian Andersen.*

The Diaries of Hans Christian Andersen.

Ellis, Alec. *A History of Children's Reading and Literature.* Oxford: Pergamon Press, 1963.

Hovde, Brynjolf Jakob. *The Scandinavian Countries 1720–1865: The Rise of the Middle Class.* Vol. 2. Ithaca: Cornell University Press, 1948.

Six

Bendix. "Hans Christian Andersen—His Methods of Amusing Children."

Hickman, Peggy. *Silhouettes, A Living Art.* Newton Abbot, Vermont: David & Charles, 1975.

*Kramer, Jack. *Silhouettes: How to Make and Use Them.* Boston: Houghton Mifflin Company, 1977.

Laliberté, Norman and Alex Mogelon. *Silhouettes, Shadows, and Cutouts.* New York: Reinhold Book Corporation, 1968.

Newman, Thelma, Jay Hartley Newman, and Lee Scott Newman. *Paper as Art and Craft: The Complete Book of the History and Processes of the Paper Arts.* New York: Crown Publishers, 1973.

Rubi, Christian. *Cut Paper, Silhouettes and Stencils: An Instruction Book.* New York: Van Nostrand Reinhold Co., 1972.

Conclusion

Böök. *Hans Christian Andersen.*

Index

DATE DUE

FOLLETT